Why I am a Spiritualist,

AND

WHY I AM NOT AN ORTHODOX.

BY

J. B. ANGELL.

WHY I AM A SPIRITUALIST,

AND

WHY I AM NOT AN ORTHODOX.

BY

J. B. ANGELL.

"Heed well the emphatic lesson of the nineteenth century, which is to thoroughly investigate a subject, however strange, before condemning it."

RED BANK, N. J.
1872.

WHY I AM A SPIRITUALIST, AND WHY I AM NOT AN ORTHODOX.

I might say, for shortness, that I am a Spiritualist because I have investigated the subject. I feel very much when I ask a person if he believes in Spiritualism and he says no, as I should if he expressed himself as not believing in the art of photography. I should say at once he had not investigated the subject. I will endeavor to give some of my experience as near as I can recollect, that has helped to confirm me in my belief.

Having lost a brother (as we generally term it) late in the spring of 1870, and being disappointed in seeing him while in his last sickness before his death, it decided me to call on some medium, and see if I could get a communication from him. I selected in my mind Mr. Charles H. Foster for the medium. But I soon learned he had gone east for the season. After his return in the fall, I called upon him at his rooms, and found him engaged with a lady and gentleman. He said to me he would soon be at liberty, and asked me to walk into the back room. I did so, and found there two ladies also waiting. Now, to get communications through Mr. Foster, he requests you to write each name of those you wish to communicate with, upon separate pieces of paper, and fold them as tight as you please, and this you can do at any time either before or after you come there. I had not written out my brother's name, and having some blank paper in my memorandum book, I thought I would write it out while I was waiting, and also added some other names I wished to communicate with at the same time. About the time I had got through, Mr. Foster came to the door for the ladies, and as they got up to walk out, one of them turned to me and says, "There is one name that you ought to have in your list that you have left out, and," says she, "his name is Thomas," asking me at the same time if I had not a friend in the spirit-world by that name. I said I could not call to mind any by that name, and asked "Was it his last name?" "O," says she, "it was his first name." Then it immediately occurred to me that I had formerly a nephew by that name. He was about my age. We grew up as it were, playmates together, and if I may judge by my own feelings, we were very much attached to each other, and it was very natural that he should have a desire to communicate with me. But he having moved out west from our native state (Rhode Island) some forty years ago, and soon having died out there, it did not occur to me to put his name on my list until reminded of it by one of the ladies, and as I was about to put his name down, the other lady says, "I saw by your side a beautiful spirit while you were writing out your list of names, and her name was Mary." And then she asked me if I had not a spirit friend by that name. Although I had that name on my list, it had for the instant slipped my mind, and as I hesitated to think, she said "Never mind, we shall see soon"; and they passed on into the front room. After I got ready (the door being left open) I could hear that they were talking upon Spiritualism, and I thought I would pass in and hear what they had to say. As I entered the room they spoke to Mr. Foster saying, "There is a gentleman [referring to me] who wishes to communicate with some of his spiritual friends, and if you have no objections, we would like to be present," and as there was none, we all sat down to a common-sized, round centre table, Mr. Foster opposite me, and the two ladies on each side of us. I put my slips of folded papers, some six or eight in number, in about the middle of the table, and soon Mr. Foster asked if there was any sprits present whose names were in those slips of paper, and there came directly three raps (apparently about the center of the table; they were about as loud as the ticking of a clock,) meaning yes, and he asked who it was. The alphabet was called for, but before we had fairly begun with the alphabet, he was impressed it was J. Angell, and immediately reached down and picked up one ef the papers and handed it to me, asking me to open it and see if that name was on it. I found it was; and soon the spirit claimed to take possession of Mr. Foster, and reaching over and grasping my hand, expressed much pleasure in meeting me, and gave a short and glowing description of their condition, surroundings, etc., in the spirit-world. Soon he left Mr. Foster and took possession of one of the ladies, and wrote a short communication to me, signing it J. A. She said "It is your father; he used to have a sore leg, and he used to limp when he walked—in this way," getting up and limping round the room, which was all true. Soon we came to Mary Angell. "There," said one of the ladies, "that is the spirit I saw standing by your side, and it is your mother." Upon opening the pellet that Mr. Foster picked up for me, as being for her, I found it was the one I put in for my mother. The first name that was called, required starting with the alphabet; immediately after a previous spirit had got through communicating, Mr. Foster would be impressed with the name of the next, and would call it, reaching down at the same time, without any hesitancy, picking up one of the papers and handing it to me to open, to see if it was correct; until he had used up all the names without making a single mistake.

Each of these spirits, after their names had been presented and investigated to see that all was correct, would take possession of Mr. Foster, and grasp me by the hand, giving me a hearty greeting, much as I should expect to receive from them if I had met them in the flesh, giving a short description of their conditions, their surroundings, and how they were enjoying themselves in their spirit-life. When it came to my brother, the principal object of my call, I asked him, among other questions, if they were settling up the business that he left in accordance with his wishes. And he said "Entirely so." And having heard from there since, I should judge that it was correct.

Now, in the foregoing, there were several quite good tests, especially from those ladies, they being entire strangers to me, never having seen or heard of them before.

Mr. Foster, after they had left, informed me that they belonged South, but came North to spend the summer, and being themselves good mediums, hence being interested in Spiritualism, and knowing of Mr. Foster by reputation as a medium, they had called upon him several times, and this was their last call before leaving for their homes South, which they expected to do next day.

Here is another test Mr. Foster gave me several years ago. After going through with my list of names as above, I told him I had heard he had the initials of spirits' names show themselves upon his arm, and he said he had, and he would ask if there were any spirits present that would communicate in that form. The response was "Yes." He immediately stripped up his sleeve leaving his arm bare; and I supposed he expected if there was anything came it would come out upon his arm. But instead of which, we soon saw it forming upon the back of his hand, and instead of its being only initials, it wrote out Susan. These letters were copper-colored (as near as I can recollect), formed upon a white hand for a base, showing a distinct contrast. They came out and remained long enough to be read and examined thoroughly, and then faded away all directly before our eyes. Says Foster, "I am impressed it was a sister of yours." It was true that I had a sister by that name, and it further occurred to me that it was like her hand-writing, and as I had some of her letters at home, I referred to them after my return and I found it to correspond, as near as I could recollect, precisely.

The first question one may naturally ask is, How were these letters formed, especially in a location we were not expecting and in an unexpected form; and how should he know I had a sister by that name; and further, how came her hand-writing there, when he could not possibly have known anything about it; and also, the form of her hand-writing had entirely passed from my mind until seeing it awakened a recollection of it.

I will give now another experience I had in connection with Mrs. Angell. This was also a number of years ago. Mrs. Angell had quite a severe ill-turn, and hearing of a medium in New York who was said to be skillful in the healing line, we decided to go over and make a trial with her. We soon found the lady. I think her name was A. W. Danworth. She was very modest and retiring in her manner, possessing a very pleasant countenance. When she got ready for the examination she said to me, "You must prepare yourself with pencil and paper for taking down the prescription when it is given, for I am entirely unconscious while under influence." The physician who claimed to prescribe through her mediumship, was named Dr. Clark, who was formerly a Thomsonian physician in Boston, and when he took possession of her, she became another kind of a person at once. She spoke up strong and confident, and walked straight up to Mrs. Angell with a staid, business air, putting her hand on Mrs. Angell's head, and commenced examining and describing her complaints, not only telling her present afflictions, but what she had been liable to at times, all without a single mistake as near as we could judge. Then she gave the prescription. After she came out of the trance, she asked Mrs. Angell if it had been satisfactory. She told her it was entirely so, as far as the examination of her complaint was concerned. Then she asked me, and I told her the same. But I said I was in hopes that we should have in connection with it some more striking tests of the truth of Spiritualism. "O," she said, "it was for one's relief, not for a test." Soon another spirit apparently took possession of her, evidently of a different character from the other, and she said, "I see standing by that lady" (meaning Mrs. Angell) "a beautiful young lady," describing her very particularly throughout. ' Although she is full-grown now, she was a child when she left the form," naming her age at that time, and how long it had been since it took place. Then she said, "I see a young man near you," describing him in like manner, and then another, and then another. "These spirits seem to take great interest in you, and call you mother. Do you recognize them as such from the description and circumstances?" As near as Mrs. Angell could recollect, it was all correct in every particular, with one exception. She never had lost but three children. "O," said the medium, "the second son was a premature birth; it never came to light alive upon your side; but he is now a young man and a beautiful spirit." This was all true—there was a premature birth took place between the two sons. Now here was a test of a very strong character. It cannot be put down as mind-reading from the medium, for Mrs. Angell could not recollect of having thought of this premature birth for years previous to this occurrence.

Since writing the above, we have had another still more vivid experience, which has just transpired with us. Having lately read in the *Banner of Light*, various accounts of extraordinary spiritual manifestations at Mr. Maurice Keeler's, near Moravia, Cayuga county, N. Y., and it being near where Mrs. Angell spent the most of her early life, and she long having had a desire to visit the scenes of her youth, with this additional inducement, it soon decided us to make a trip there for our two-fold gratification.

We went directly to Mr. Keeler's house, which is about half a mile from the village, upon ground so high that the vilage of Moravia appears, as it were, nestling at our feet, and this, with the valley for miles beyond, presents a view that is rarely excelled for its beauty. On our first day's arrival, there were so many people there before us that we did not succeed in attending a circle. After which we attended four. But in the three first there was nothing occurred that was of especial interest to us. The room in which we formed was darkened most of the time, so that in going in to form a circle, we had to take a light with us, and in arranging us in a semicircular form, some eight or ten people just fills out the space from one side of the room to the other, all taking hold of each other's hands, some six or eight feet in front of the medium, who sits with her back near the cabinet. No one can get into the circle, except they come through the cabinet, without getting over the circle's heads. After the circles are formed, the light is turned down, leaving the circle in utter darkness. In the fourth circle that we attended, we had eight persons, seven of them old people, I should judge over sixty years, and one middle-aged. It is understood that singing aids in giving harmony and strength to the manifesting powers. Our circle of mainly old people was not especially blessed with very exalted singing talent, but I believe we all put in the best we knew. Old John Brown seemed to have the most awakening power among the spirits while we were there, and we soon struck in upon that, and we had not proceeded far before there was evidence of magnetic power about us. Little mild, bluish lights began to circulate about over our heads, and over the space just in front of us for a time, and then vanished. Then each member of the circle was consecrated by a holy sprinkling in our faces. Then there joined us in the chorus a spirit man's voice, singing the treble, and soon a second man's voice, singing the tenor; and directly they joined us, soon after we commenced, carrying their two separate parts through the whole song, including the chorus, and when we had used up all the words we knew, they improvised words for us that none of the circle ever heard before. At one time an additional spirit lady's voice joined us, and sung her part through with the other two spirits. These voices did not apparently come from a stationary point while singing, but seemed to be waving about in the upper part of the room, some of the time nearly over our heads, and at other times over the space just in front of us. Their voices were of the richest, and of the truest ring. It seemed to stir every fibre of one's musical soul. No mundane effort that I ever witnessed would compare with it for its exhilarating effect. In due time a spirit man's voice spoke directly in front of us, saying, "Please strike the light." These introductory circles are formed, they say, in the dark, with the mediums seated outside of the cabinet to establish strong manifesting power. The lamp is lit, and placed upon the piano, on one side of the room, behind a screen that shades it from the main part of the room, but allows it to shine obliquely upon a small black, curtained window in the front part of the cabinet. The window is all open, excepting the curtain. After this the medium takes her seat in the cabinet, and the person that lights the lamp and shuts the door after the medium, returns to his seat in the circle as before. Then the circle commenced singing again, but we got no more aid from the spirits. The power seemed to be wanted in another direction. Our feeble efforts in this line, after having been exhilarated with such a glorious accompaniment from such a heavenly quarter, seemed a pretty tame affair, I assure you. Nevertheless, as long as we felt that our exertions were of any service, we rendered them to the best of our capacity. Soon the curtain began to rise, and several faces presented themselves in succession at the cabinet window, but none of the circle could recognize them with any certainty. Finally a lady seemed to be making efforts to bring her face forward, and at last succeeded in bringing it out to the light, and it was recognized with delight at once by an elderly lady in the circle. This elderly lady made some remark to her (the import of which I have forgotten), to which the spirit assented by giving three very graceful inclinations of the head. The spirit's whole deportment seemed easy and very graceful. She had a very fine countenance, with apparently fine wavy brown hair combed down over her temples, with a band around her head, and a small ornament at the centre of the parting, which sparkled as the light shone upon it. She was formerly the wife of one of the hotel keepers at Auburn, with whom the elderly lady said she had been familiarly acquainted with for years previous to her leaving the form, and said, while she was living, ease and gracefulness of movement was characteristic of her. That same evening, after this circle, we left for Auburn, accompanied by the above lady, and we stopped at the same hotel where this spirit-lady while in the form used to live, and we were invited into the hotel keeper's family sitting-room to see a large-sized photograph of her, and a striking resembance was recognized at once. There were the same noble features, the parted hair coming down over her temples, apparently resembling in every particular, the one we had seen but a few hours before, bowing so gracefully to us at the cabinet window at Mr. Keeler's.

Directly a man's face was seen coming up, and the moment the light struck it so that its features could be seen, it gave Mrs. Angell such a shock that she could scarcely contain herself in her seat, for the features were apparently precisely those of a living son of hers, and the first thought was that he had left the form since she had heard from him, and took this opportunity to make himself manifest. Then it occurred to her it might be one of her sons that she had lost; and she said, "Is it Samuel?" There was no response. She said, "Is it John?" This was assented to at once, by an inclination of the head. "O," she said, "if it is John, will you speak?" and he pushed his face out to the light, a smile lit up his countenance, simply saying at the same time, "Mother"; and his lips wereplainly seen to move when he spoke the word; after being requested to say more, he said, "Mother, I am with you every day." Then after something further was stated, the import of which I have forgotten, his answer was, "Your impressions are correct." Then a lady's hand was presented, with three fingers partly gone, which a lady present recognized at once as her sister's hand, who passed over some years ago.

Then an old lady, with a very broad bordered white cap upon her head, tried several times to come up to the light, and finally succeeded; but the border of her cap was so broad, and projected so far over her face, that the light could not shine upon her countenance so as to discover her features. She presented her face towards the part of the circle where I was, and she was asked which one of us she wished to communicate with, and she pointed with her finger toward me. Then I asked her who she was, and she said, "Your Granny Angell." Then I asked her if she would say something more, and she said, "It is very hard work for us to talk now, but the time is soon coming when we can talk with each other freely." Grandmother Angell left the form nearly or quite sixty years ago, when I was probably some four or five years old, at which time, old women of her age used to wear just such caps as she presented herself with, and it was the custom among children in the country, where we lived at that time, to call our grand-parents on the female side, Grannies. In her latter days, she lived with my father's family, occupying a room in the second story, and being too old and feeble to go down stairs, her meals used to be taken up to her ; excepting some simple things, which, when her health would permit, she used to cook herself. And as I was some seven years younger than any of the rest of the family, and for the want of more appropriate material, I presume I used to be to some extent a favorite of hers; for I recollect from time to time she invited me to take my meals with her, and those johnny-cakes that she used to bake upon a board, propped up upon one edge by a flat iron, on the hearth before a wood fire, had a sweetness in them that none of our stove-baked, modern corn-bread family approaches to. All things considered, it was not strange that she should make herself manifest to her now old but once young (perhaps) pet boy. Especially when doing so makes the test more perfect, for among all my connections and friends that I had flattered myself I might see, the possibility of my Grandmother Angell, whose absence from her old body had been of so long standing, had not entered my mind as one who might present herself to me. Hence it could not be put down as clairvoyant mind-reading of the medium.

Now here is a line of tests that seem to me are beyond the possibility of being accounted for, excepting through the return of spirit-friends. No combination of talent in the legerdemain line could present at that window likenesses of friends that are readily recognized by members of the circle, some of whom are entire strangers, not only to the Keelers and the medium, but to every other member of the circle.

But for Mr. and Mrs. Keeler and the medium to accomplish so much through any peculiar art of theirs, would be still wonderfully more strange, for I think of all my acquaintances, from my boyhood up, I cannot call to mind any that would appear so illy qualified for carrying out a line of deception as Mr. and Mrs. Keeler.

The medium is more easy, and not so awkward in her manner, but apparently entirely honest and sincere in her deportment.

Tests in multitudes, and of various forms, (for there are no two just alike) are occurring throughout this and other countries daily, many of them of such a conclusive character that I am entirely satisfied that any appreciative mind, whose judgment is not controlled by his prejudices, his feelings, or his fears, and who will faithfully investigate the subject, he will receive evidence of such a conclusive nature that conviction will unavoidably follow. For when we have received evidence sufficient of the truth of a thing, our convictions follow in spite of ourselves. One might from strong prejudice, perhaps, resist coming in contact with the evidence that there is, under certain conditions, a power in steam for propelling machinery. But when he allows himself to take an appreciative view of its workings, he has to ground arms, strike his colors, and surrender to his convictions.

The question is sometimes asked, Of what use is Spiritualism ? I feel that the scope of its uses are not easily measured. We will take this last case of Mrs. Angell. What a thrill of joy must come over a loving mother's feelings, when such vivid evidence was presented to her understanding of the glorious condition of those, the parting with which left a void that seemed to be a hopeless case to be closed in this life at least. But this brought a conviction with it that they not only still lived, but that they still took an earnest interest in their mother; and further, that when she had stayed her time out here, and passed over, she would meet them under the full appreciation of a mother's feelings (only, as it is stated, more vividly there than here).

Again, this settles the question which so agitates the world, and upon which there are so many doubters and utter unbelievers. Do we live hereafter or is the soul immortal ?

Then again, I have seen it stated that there are some sixty thousand ministers in the United States alone, and as I understand it, what is expected of a minister different from other public teachers, is that he is to minister for the good of our souls, or that he is to set forth the evidences of a future life, and how we must conduct ourselves to attain the best conditions in that life. Now, in my estimation, an intelligent person, with a good medium, under proper conditions, can get more facts about our condition hereafter in a few hours, than the whole sixty thousand ministers can give us (without this aid) in their life-time, and this, too, without ruffling a hair of their heads. These are a few of the items out of the many I might name, which I feel are of themselves of no small interest, and may give a hint of the good we may expect from Spiritualism.

Another natural question further to ask is, What doctrine does Spiritualism teach? It teaches emphatically the doctrine of doing unto others as you would that they should do unto you, and loving your neighbor as yourself; and he who lives the nearest to these principles, attains a condition the nearest heaven, or a heavenly state of existence, and he does not have to wait for it until he passes over. It begins here. For when is a person nearer heaven than when he has done a noble, kind, and just act to his neighbor? and when is he nearer hell than when he has done a mean, unjust, and cruel act to his neighbor? This is the real heaven and hell so much talked about. This burning, liquid, brimstone hell, with its accompanying personal Devil, *is all a myth.* There are none so low but that they will be redeemed, and each has got to perform his own redemption himself. No one can do it for him any more than he can eat, drink, or sleep for him, and if he does not begin his reformation here, he will have to sometime hereafter, and his punishment will be just in proportion to the evil he has committed.

You may readily imagine that some have a heavy load to struggle up through, but there are none free. All are far, very far, from perfection. Progress is the grand ruling principle both here and hereafter, and every step forward in that direction produces its own glorious reward. And there is room in that direction for all, from the lowest to the highest.

These are some, as I suppose, of what may be called the doctrinal ideas of Spiritualism.

Now, of course, believing as I do in the truth of Spiritualism, it is a sufficient reason of itself why I am not an Orthodox. But there are other reasons, which I will try to explain, why I am not a believer in the so-called Orthodox principles.

As I understand it, all who do not live up to their particular form, as laid down in their various creeds, are lost. And the opinion of people differ about the proportion of those that are lost. Some say nine-tenths, others nineteen-twentieths, ninety-nine-hundreths, etc.; but by statistics the proportion, I think, can be more satisfactorily approximated to. It is estimated that the number of inhabitants on the globe is some ten hundred millions, and that one-third of this number are under the Christian dominions, and that the proportion of actual members of some church throughout the Christian countries, averages some say one-fourth, others one-fifth, of the people, which former proportion foots up some eighty-three millions of people that are actual members of some church, which is about one-twelfth of the race. [If my statistics are not entirely correct, if the actual proportion should be more, or less, mind you it would only alter the degree, not the principle in the least.] The result of which is, there cannot, according to the Orthodox idea, be but one in twelve of the human family saved.

Is it possible that a power that could call into existence suns upon suns, and worlds upon worlds, poised in space perhaps millions deep, and all moving with such precision, order, and justice, towards each other, that an eclipse can be calculated a thousand years ahead with entire certainty of its taking place at its appointed time; and if we may judge other worlds by our own, the apparent object of this grand effort is to mature man and prepare him for a future state of existence: (for in man is represented all beings below him; in addition to which, is his own superior intelligence; and he is the only being of earth who possesses the religious idea, who entertains an aspiration for a future state of existence;—evidently man is the culminating fruit of this immense forest of worlds, the harvesting of which is to fill the spiritual granaries of heaven;) is it possible, I say, that a power that can direct all this with such apparent ease and order, should make such a melancholy mistake? the result of which is that only one in twelve should be saved, the other eleven-twelfths of the race to be lost—yes, infinitely as it were, worse than lost, for they will have to undergo the most excruciating torment throughout eternity.

The Orthodox idea, as I understand it, is that we must realize a change of heart through Christ to be saved. Now two-thirds of the inhabitants of the globe are what we term heathens, a great portion of which never heard of Christ, many of them probably living as near to the Golden Rule as it is possible for human nature to come up to, devoting their lives to doing good, ever rendering relief to the suffering of those about them, and when their lives are spent, and their bodies are cast off, they find their spirits doomed to eternal misery for the neglect of attending to certain forms, the necessity of which never came to their knowledge, and there was no possible chance for them to obtain that knowledge. Is that just? Is it merciful? Is it reasonable? If it was possible for man to commit such a deed, would it not be considered a crime of the deepest dye, and can we familiarize ourselves with such deep injustice, without its having its unfavorable influence upon us ? Was not the condition of the South a striking illustration of the contaminating influence of unjust surroundings ? The effect of slavery had so toned down their moral standard that they proclaimed it a divine institution, and each popular denomination was represented there by scores of ministers, preaching from their pulpits the divinity of slavery. When we came to fight with the South, we found that they were capable of deeds below what we should expect from barbarians—such as murdering our soldiers after they had surrendered, and starving them, while in their power as prisoners, by thousands directly under the eyes, as it were, and in the full knowledge of their Confederate Congress, hence evidently showing it to have been a national policy. The poet has it when he says,

Vice is a monster, of such a frightful mein,
That to be hated needs but to be seen;
But seen too oft, with too familiar a face,
We first endure, then pity, then embrace.

Now, kind reader, I do not give the above reflections in a spirit of controversy, but in the spirit I should expect from you, if it should be that I was a skeptic upon magnetic telegraphing, and had expressed myself to that effect. But finally, when the evidence had been presented to me so directly that I could not deny the fact, but had to admit it, I then pronounced it all the work of the devil, and hence would have nothing to do with it; if I had any messages to send, I would send them in the old way, by a relay of horses and their riders; now, in the best of feeling, you would try to impress me of my mistake ; perhaps by stating that there was one company in New York who had 121,000 miles of wire, over which, under proper conditions, they could send messages more miles in a few hours, than perhaps 60,000 horses with their riders could carry in their life-time, and this, too, without ruffling a hair of their heads. What would be your feelings, if at this stage, I should commence deriding and stigmatizing you and your idea to the utmost of my capacity? You would naturally say to yourself, how gross, how unjust, and uncivil a return for an intended kindness —a kindness in which you had directly no possible interest except for my good. How often is Spiritualism and its advocates assailed in like manner from Orthodox quarters? But then it is all in keeping. It would be folly to expect a stream to flow higher than its fountain.

There is one other point I wish to illustrate by magnetic telegraphing. The truth of telegraphing, as with Spiritualism, is sustained by present living facts, not upon some ancient record of events, that transpired some two, four, or five thousand years ago; but facts that are transpiring daily and hourly all about us. Here is one of the important advantages it has over every other heretofore professed doctrine. Backsliders are very rare from convictions obtained through present, positive, living evidence. Professor Morse does not find it necessary every few months to go round frightening back into his fold backsliders from his magnetic faith; but, upon the contrary, he might travel the world through, and he would find every intelligent member of the race a fast subscriber to his doctrine, without a single dissenter. It is said if the Spiritualist doctrine is a doctrine of love, why do we see among them at their meetings at times, such a want of harmony? Now do not expect too much at once. A change perhaps in belief from a God of wrath and injustice to a just and merciful God, is not sure to change the character of the individual at once. The long ages of the demoralizing influence of slavery was not changed the moment that Lincoln proclaimed the freedom of the slaves, of which the existence of the Ku Kluxes and their kindred spirits are a conclusive evidence. Strong biased minds can only be changed by long, patient, earnest training.

We hear much said at times, in certain quarters, about evangelizing the world; and the leaders perhaps of some leading denomination, will get their heads together to work up a powerful revival in view of that object. Now what do these revivals amount to? It appears to me (to use a homely comparison), it is like applying soda wash to the stalk and branches of a sickly tree; you may get up a fitful semblance for a time of vivid life, but if the grub worm of injustice is left girdling at the roots, the whole tree in time will surely perish.

Talk about evangelizing the world. If it is a fact, as the Bible says, that we commenced with a single pair some five or six thousand years ago, and we know now that we count up in round numbers some ten hundred millions, it is no wise probable but that the last third of this five or six thousand years has gained fully its portion of the ten hundred millions. Hence, while the race has been gaining at least three hundred and thirty-three millions, Christianity has only gained some eighty-three millions. Now it does not require a very deep mathematician, to perceive that upon this ratio it would take a long time to evangelize the world.

The *Banner of Light* sometime since contained an account of the proceedings of the Massachusetts Legislative Committee, which was appointed, it seems, to investigate the propriety of allowing the Spiritualists a special charter like other denominations for publishing tracts advocating their doctrines. I see, according to the statement, three of the Committee were ministers, and I should judge from the tone of their questions, they were of the Orthodox order, and it would seem that their great fear was that the Spiritualist had too little reverence for the Bible. Now the contents of the Bible are of such a varied cast, that all shades of doctrine can find passages that can be plausibly construed to sustain them; and they have only to say, as the custom is, that all other parts of it that opposes their particular standard are figurative, and theirs is the true literal meaning. Hence, the Universalist will perhaps call your attention to the passage where it says, "As in Adam all die, even so in Christ shall all be made alive." The Shaker will probably tell you it is good to marry, but better to not; therefore they take the better part. The Mormons will quote you David, a man after God's own heart, to sustain them. And the slaveholders used to find passages which they felt fully sustained their institution. And the Orthodox finds ample evidence there, as they understand it, to sustain eternal suffering to all outside of their creeds. And even John Allen, the wickedest man in New York, I presume used to think that the life of old King Solomon was a mantle sufficiently large to amply cover his leading iniquitous deeds; and it was said of him that in his controversies he used generally to come out master of the occasion. In the above light, the Bible (with those who believe in the peculiar sacredness of its contents,) acts, as it were, as a moral thermometer, showing as a rule quite plainly, how high each denominational moral mercury stands above zero. What can be said of the moral standard of a class of people who profess to be followers of Christ, the spirit of whose life and teachings, as recorded, were to love thy neighbor as thyself, return good for evil, if a man smite you on one cheek turn the other also, and instead of adhering to these high and holy precepts they search the Bible up and down for evidences of a god of vengeance, wrath, and retaliation, and when found they sieze and quote them with a gusto, showing plainly that it touches a kindred spirit in their own mental organization; for although, as I said, they are directly opposed to the whole life and teachings of Christ, these extreme retaliatory passages must be absorbed in their creeds, or it will not seem a truth to them.

Spiritualism is like the light of the sun; it shines to us in its own natural way independent of our control. Our heretofore denominations are like our various artificial lights, each individual or class choosing its particular light, according to its fancy or capacity for its support, each light shining in its own flickering, sickly way, for the few just about it. But Spiritualism, I say furthermore, like the sun, shines for all. Not a soul is born but what in time will be a joyful recipient of its glorious rays.

Is it not plain, if they were brought to the test, which of the two above classes would be most likely to adopt the extreme policy of our southern brethren heretofore mentioned. For what is the transcient suffering of a starving or murdered man, compared with an eternity of misery, each moment of which is infinitely as it were greater than that of the man while being robbed of the life of his body, even in its most aggravated form, and this punishment, too, must be endured in many cases merely because his conscience perhaps would not permit him to subscribe to the thirty-nine (more or less) articles of faith ? For he might be the most exalted pattern of a man for justice, truth, and love to his neighbor; but if he fails to subscribe to the Orthodox creed an eternity of misery is his inevitable doom.

And this is the class that enlightened Massachusetts, through its enlightened representatives, voted that Spiritualists should not be allowed equal advantages for promulgating its doctrines.

And this is the leading class whose minds are so terribly exercised for fear Spiritualism will demoralize the race.

And, also, among this class, are those who are so earnest for our return to the old form of Church and State—a condition of things, which was so severely felt by Roger Williams, when he had to flee for his life from the old Colony of Massachusetts over to Rhode

Island among the desperate Narragansetts, for his conscience sake; also by the so-called witches, who were executed at Salem; by the Quakers, who were hung on Boston Common; by John Rogers, who was burned at the stake in old Smithfield; and was it not for the fact, that since then a mighty change has come over its surroundings, and had Orthodoxy of the old school the power, free from the fear of the influence of these surroundings, could we expect a better state of things now than then? Could we even yet expect a stream to flow higher than its fountain?

The question will naturally be asked, if Orthodoxy is such a terrible affair, How comes it that so many of the reforms have come through its church? Has it not been so as far back as we know of the race. Doubtless each step up the rounds of the ladder of progress could truthfully say that upon their particular round had been established the greatest reforms that had taken place previous to their time; but did that prove that they had attained perfection? Here has been and is the great stumbling-block. Each considers his platform the ultimate of all progress, the highest round in the ladder. And this to, when it is plain that our wisest are, infinitely as it were, more below perfection than our veriest idiots are below our wisest; therefore, what consummate presumption to say that we are perfect in any important direction. It seems to be our nature to insist upon wearing our old swaddling cloths, even after our mental and moral limbs are away in advance struggling for greater freedom. How ridiculous would be the position of the chicken, while being fully decked out in Nature's elegant plumage, if it should insist upon carrying its old shell upon its back, because at some previous time perhaps it had been so well served by it.

There is many a member of the Orthodox church whose soul is all aglow with a beautiful, high-toned, moral, and religious plumage, who make a wofully ridiculous figure by insisting upon wearing on their backs the old Orthodox shell.

I fully believe that all the doctrines that have heretofore existed, from Old Brahma up, have been in the main founded upon speculation. Hence each individual, as a rule, would be attracted to the doctrine that accorded most with his or her mental organization. And as there are no two organized just alike, therefore the existence of the great multiplicity of doctrines is entirely natural, each showing the condition or status of the mind, each doubtless filling its niche in the line of progress, acting, as it were, as caustics to burn the proud flesh out of the old religious sore, preparatory for the reception of the healing ointment of Spiritualism.

I presume at this stage the unprejudiced, intelligent reader may perceive why I am not an Orthodox.

Now, it appears to me that in the foregoing I have, in the main, stated plain, self-evident facts. If so, facts are mighty staid and reliable articles to deal with. They are as permanent as the rocks—aye, more so. You might roll up a pile of the hardest granite as high as the Andes, or the Himelaya Mountains—in time they would dissolve and moulder to dust. But a truth, *Never.*

PHALANX, N. J.

www.ingramcontent.com/pod-product-compliance
Lightning Source LLC
LaVergne TN
LVHW011142110826
845150LV00008B/2470

* 9 7 8 1 4 1 8 1 9 2 6 7 9 *